TINY TREASURES

BY JODIE BIVENS

© 2023 Jodie Bivens
All rights reserved.

Scripture quotations marked (AMP) and (AMPC) are taken from the Amplified Bible, Copyright © 2015 by The Lockman Foundation. Used by permission.

Scripture quotations marked (CSB) have been taken from the Christian Standard Bible®, Copyright © 2017 by Holman Bible Publishers. Used by permission. Christian Standard Bible® and CSB® are federally registered trademarks of Holman Bible Publishers.

Scripture quotations marked (ESV) are taken from The ESV® Bible (The Holy Bible, English Standard Version®), © 2001 by Crossway, a publishing ministry of Good News Publishers. Used by permission. All rights reserved.

Scripture quotations marked (NIV) are taken from the Holy Bible, New International Version®, NIV®. Copyright © 1973, 1978, 1984, 2011 by Biblica, Inc.™ Used by permission of Zondervan. All rights reserved worldwide. www.zondervan.com. The "NIV" and "New International Version" are trademarks registered in the United States Patent and Trademark Office by Biblica, Inc.™

Scripture quotations marked (TLB) are taken from The Living Bible, copyright © 1971 by Tyndale House Foundation. Used by permission of Tyndale House Publishers, Carol Stream, Illinois 60188. All rights reserved.

Scripture quotations marked (THE MESSAGE) are taken from THE MESSAGE. Copyright © 1993, 1994, 1995, 1996, 2000, 2001, 2002. Used by permission of NavPress Publishing Group.

Edited by Danny May

TABLE OF CONTENTS

Foreword by Tasha Layton vii
Introduction 1
Day 1:   Encouraging Another 4
Day 2:   Backseat Lessons 8
Day 3:   PDA 12
Day 4:   Manic Monday 16
Day 5:   5:22 20
Day 6:   Grown 24
Day 7:   Sweet Saturday 28
Day 8:   The Gift of Giving 32
Day 9:   Super Uber 36
Day 10: The Table 40
Day 11: Hold Your Torch High 44
Day 12: Say It 48
Day 13: Joyful Anticipation 52
Day 14: Imperfections 56
Day 15: Good Mascara Day 60
Day 16: Don't Waste the Moment 64
Day 17: Self-Grace 68
Day 18: My Swiss Army Knife 72
Day 19: Fulfillment in a Good No 76
Day 20: Morning Hums 80

Day 21: Just Say, "Thank You" 84
Day 22: Maturing Up 88
Day 23: Divine Intervening 92
Day 24: Healed Hurt 96
Day 25: Sunrise & Sunset 100
Day 26: Royalty in Loyalty 104
Day 27: Good Company 108
Day 28: Temples and Thrones 112
Day 29: Redisplay 116
Day 30: Make Every Effort 120
Day 31: Black Eyes & Little Lies 124
Day 32: Happy With It 128
Day 33: One Thousand Times 132
Day 34: Noticed 136
Day 35: He Didn't Know How to be Mean 140
Day 36: From Fatter to Father 144
Day 37: Home 148
Day 38: Love Wins 152
Day 39: God Stories 156
Day 40: From That Time On 160

FOREWORD

When I think of Jodie Bivens, I think of the love of Christ. It was my honor to get to know Jodie when I was a worship leader in Kentucky, and since that time, I have seen how contagious, free, and worshipful her spirit is. She is a joy to be around, and her passion for praising God has the potential to unlock a similar joy in others. Jodie has the special ability to see the beauty of God's blessing in every day and every person—and now she is sharing that gift with us in the form of her devotional, Tiny Treasures.

At times, we all get caught up in the busyness of life. It's natural to focus on the next shiny object, the next deadline, the next item to check off the to-do list. But Tiny Treasures reminds us that we can find God's glory and beauty amid the everyday moments of life, if only we remember to look for them. When we aim our thoughts in the direction of gratitude, our hearts will follow suit. Soon we will see things we once overlooked and be overcome by the surprises of even the smallest joys hiding within each day.

Since reading Jodie's devotional, I've sought out those tiny treasures in my own life. And let me tell you, the practice has made such an impact. Jodie's words have encouraged me to stay positive in my daily pursuits, and I can't begin to tell you how grateful I am for that. I pray that you, too, will discover the small wonders that surround you each day. By looking for God's good hand in all things, we will find our spirits and our perspectives truly transformed.

Jodie herself is a treasure to so many, and her devotions can inspire us all to take the time to cherish every gift from above. May her words bless you over the coming days, and may each tiny treasure become a reminder of God's unfailing, unchanging love.

–Christian singer, songwriter, and author, Tasha Layton

INTRODUCTION

Hey there!

It's so good to see you in the pages of Tiny Treasures. I hope you are doing well. Let me introduce you to the inspiration behind the devotion. It all started with one word.

Every January I pick a word to focus on throughout the year. In the year of 2022, the word for me was treasure. I borrowed it from Mary in Luke 2:19 & 51. Here, we see her treasuring her moments. One was a joyful moment of birth and the other came after a fearful moment of losing her son then finding him in his Father's House. Joyful or frustrated, she treasured the moments in her heart.

I had noticed a continual pattern of just going through my days without really paying attention to the little things that were truly valuable. This word, treasure, made me focus on the everyday good things that I sometimes overlooked. As I recognized these moments, I wanted to hold onto them before they slipped away into yesterday. So, I decided that each night before bed, I would think back through my day, hunting for any moment I may have missed or any tiny treasure that I might have skipped right past. As I thought through them, I would write them down. I had a small unused notebook in a drawer that I started using to journal my thoughts and titled it "Tiny Treasures 2022".

Every single night, all 365 of them, I sat on my bed and thought through the day I was about to lay to rest. I would close my eyes to remember the small victories, the frustrations, the laughs, the disappointments, the blessings, and I would write down three things in this little journal of gratitude. I also made a photo album in my phone's gallery to have a visible reminder of a lot of these treasures. In the public world of social media, I didn't post a lot that year. Mary pondered her treasures in her heart, not on social media to be bragged or complained about. She found meaning in both the ups and the downs. That was my goal for the entire year.

This is how the book you are holding in your hands was born. After a year of writing in my journal, a dream I had always carried started to emerge out of the shadows – to write a devotional book. These devotionals are just highlights of the tiny treasures I found that might bring you inspiration to find the tiny treasures of your day. There are a few inspirations that my boys wrote too, and that makes me happy that they participated with me in this book.

My prayer for this book, as you find encouragement and humor through some of my treasures, is that you'll ponder the treasures of your own heart and write them down in the pages provided for you each day. It's meant to be done at night as you reflect on your day. This type of reflection is actually a practice that started in the 1500's, called the daily Examen. It's about tracing our steps and finding worth in all the moments of our day; the small ones as much as the big ones.

Ready to start searching?

DAY 1

For they have refreshed my spirit and yours. Therefore, recognize such people.

1 CORINTHIANS 16:18 (CSB)

ENCOURAGING ANOTHER

Tiny treasures. That's what I wanted to find. Not just tiny treasures, but tiny God-treasures. I wanted my mind, my eyes, and my heart to be aware of the goodness around me in that day. Like the sunrise, the silliness of my boys, or just that I had a good day at work. What I didn't expect to find was the goodness of a fellow coworker.

Sitting across the room, I listened to the kindness in her voice and patience in her posture as she worked with a customer. Her endurance to be calm and listen resonated with me and I wanted her to know I noticed. I was really wishing I had a sheet of gold star stickers, but since I didn't, I got resourceful. Taking a yellow highlighter, I drew a bright yellow star on a piece of scrap paper and cut it out. There's never a bad time for arts and crafts. Once I cut it out and put a piece of tape on the back, I walked it over to her desk and stuck it on her computer and told her everything I had just seen in her and her awesomeness deserved a gold star.

It remains on her computer to this day.

Paul tells us in 1 Corinthians 16:30 to recognize people who refresh our spirits.

There have been times that I failed at giving recognition. I've seen beauty in a friend and let the thought pass. I've been amazed by the wisdom in a coworker yet walked away. I've noticed talent in a stranger, but I just kept going by. What if I had simply paused and let these people know how much they blessed me?

Finding a tiny treasure isn't about digging around for our own riches; tiny treasures can be discovered in the beauty of someone else. What makes it a treasure is when we tell that person what we see. The encouragement that shines through their eyes—just because you notice them and take the time to recognize it—not only brings joy to them, but also to you.

Lord, I pray for eyes to see the beauty in another. When my focus is stuck inward may You draw me outward and away from myself. And thank you that I can quickly order a sheet of gold star stickers from Amazon.

Amen!

TODAY'S TREASURES

DAY 2

Is anyone among you in trouble? Let them pray. Is anyone happy? Let them sing songs of praise.

JAMES 5:13 (NIV)

BACKSEAT LESSONS

I've never considered it fun to go through situations that didn't work out as easy as I had hoped. There are times when I just want to get something accomplished, but I get frustrated at myself for not performing good enough, or for not getting it done sooner, or that my pace is slower than most. I have a hard time remembering the journey itself is more important than the destination. I simply want it to be done and say, "Okay, situation, you made your point. I've learned it already. Can we just move on?"

The success of accomplishing tasks, or learning new ways to do things, may depend on our attitude.

Not too long ago, I got a backseat view to someone who was going through a situation that wasn't as easy as he hoped. Our middle son was learning to drive. Although parallel parking didn't naturally come easy to him, I noticed his countenance seemed different from my own when in the middle of accomplishing a task. I watched as he listened to his dad and followed his instructions. Then, in a moment of silence, he started to sing. He sang along with the song playing on the radio in complete calm and comfort. In the middle of learning I noticed his confidence. It was in his ability to be comfortable that I treasured his state of happiness.

In chapter 5, James writes several verses encouraging us to be patient in suffering. In verse 13, he answers two questions. First,

"Is anyone among you in trouble? Let them pray." Second, "Is anyone happy? Let them sing songs of praise." Prayer should always be my natural starting point when I'm in a trial, just like singing should be a common response to the happiness God provides me every day. Yet, so often, I get stuck in my overthinking and tune out my Father's grace-filled instructions.

I don't know if Isaiah even realized he was singing that day. He was just being himself while in the middle of learning. I do know he doesn't realize how much I learned in that backseat moment, but it was the best seat for me to learn from him.

Lord, thank you for lessons learned from the backseat. May we learn to make a joyful noise from any seat we find ourselves in. Help us to be grateful for our pace, enjoying the scenery along the way.
Amen!

TODAY'S TREASURES

DAY 3

She was forgiven many, many sins, and so she is very, very grateful.

LUKE 7:47 (THE MESSAGE)

PDA

I still recall the first worship song I ever heard, because it was the first song of the first real worship service that I had ever been a part of. The song was, Our God is an Awesome God. It was August 1998, and I was 20 years old. At the time, words like worship, praise, repentance, or salvation were not a part of my vocabulary. I wouldn't have known how to use them in a sentence when it came to Christianity.

I was visiting my big brother for a couple weeks and he took me to the youth group he was leading at the time. I had never been to anything like it. I remember looking around during that first worship service and taking it all in. I saw teenagers lift their arms and hands into the air, singing, and being excited.

As that first Wednesday night came to an end, Our God is an Awesome God was played again to close out the service. This time, I found my lips moving along with the lyrics. It was easy to sing because it didn't have a lot of words.

The following Wednesday rolled around. I don't truly remember what my brother spoke about that night (sorry bro), but I remember the altar call he gave. Once again, the band started playing Our God is an Awesome God softly in the background. Something began to stir in my heart. It was beating fast. Tears began to stream down my face, and I lifted my hands and arms! As my brother proceeded with the altar call, my feet took two large steps forward and my sister-in-law prayed a prayer with me. For the first time ever, I felt the love and acceptance of Jesus and I have never been the same since.

I believe from that moment on, I was forgiven. All I had to offer Jesus that night was my sin-stained life, yet He took it and washed it clean. He took it like He took the widow's penny and treated it like it was gold.

This is why I treasure worship and the reason I put my whole heart into worship. It's why I display such affection for Him and to Him. It's why I let myself get undignified for Him. I raise my hands! I jump around! I clap and sing really loud because I love Him, but more than that, because He loved me first. He loved me IN MY SIN! I've never been more grateful for anything like I'm grateful for my salvation, His forgiveness, and His love.

Public displays of affection (PDA) are acts of physical intimacy in the view of others. Intimacy doesn't have to be what we initially make it out to be in our gutter minds. Intimacy is a familiarity or a friendship. I'm familiar with Jesus because I spend time with Him every day. He knows everything about me – the good, the bad, and the ugly. I feel connected to Him and supported by Him. I can be emotional around Him. Through worship, I can bring all these feelings to Him. It is through worship that I focus on Jesus and center everything on Him. All my stress and worries melt away in those moments. It's just me and Jesus together, in worship – a public display of affection.

Lord, thank you for the freedom found in worship. I will give you my whole self in worship because you gave your whole self to me.
Amen!

TODAY'S TREASURES

DAY 4

Haven't I commanded you: be strong and courageous? Do not be afraid or discouraged, for the Lord your God is with you wherever you go.

JOSHUA 1:9 (CSB)

MANIC MONDAY

One more big stretch. One more big yawn. Just five more minutes, because I'm the most comfortable I've been all night. Then, it happens. ALARM! It's time to get up.

It's Monday morning. The start of a new week. In many workplaces, Mondays are the busiest and usually the most dreaded day. It's the day you don't want to get out of bed. The day you plan to wear comfy shoes. The day you want that extra cup of coffee. The day you start counting down to the next weekend. Ironically, as much I wish Monday was just an extension of Sunday, one thing I've come to realize: I haven't died on a Monday yet.

After a year of writing every night in my own Tiny Treasures journal, the second most-mentioned treasure I wrote was making it through Mondays. What if I didn't live each day just waiting for the weekend though? Instead of being thankful I made it through a Monday, what if I saw the opportunity of a new week? What if I lived out the words God gave to Joshua, "be strong and courageous and not be discouraged," knowing I can handle whatever Monday throws at me because God is with me every day.

After much practice, and it'll still require more practice, I'm treasuring that I woke up for another Monday. Changing my mindset from, "I have to go to work" to, "I get to go to work." I'm sure Joshua could have dreaded the huge task of trying to fill

Moses' shoes by being appointed the new leader of Gods' people. Yet, the Bible shows no signs of dread. He just displayed trust and obedience in the task laid out before him.

Joshua led the Israelites to the promise land in his own shoes. We may see the weekend as an upcoming promise land, but joy can still come in the morning of every day—including Mondays.

After all, Mondays are what we make of them.

―――――――――――――――――――――――――

Lord, thank you for each day you give us. May we make the most of our daily dose of grace, knowing You are with us wherever we go.
Amen!

TODAY'S TREASURES

DAY 5

"If you keep silent at this time, relief and deliverance will come to the Jewish people from another place, but you and your father's family will be destroyed. Who knows, perhaps you have come to your royal position for such a time as this."

ESTHER 4:14 (CSB)

5:22

Don't you just love a good God hug? Not a friendly side hug, bro hug, or quick-pat-on-the-back hug. I'm talking about a full-on, squeeze-your-guts-out-because-I-love-you-so-much-and-want-you-to-know-it hug. This may sound super cheesy, but anytime I happen to look at the clock and it says 5:22 I feel like God is hugging me like that.

You see, I was born May 22nd, so when I see 5:22, I feel like He is reminding me that He chose for me to be born on that specific day for His specific purpose. For such a time as this, He loves me. He has good things in store for me. Yes, there are also trials in store for me and I have already walked through some, but I didn't walk through them alone. He was always with me. Nothing is a surprise to Him because He has gone before me. He knew the day I would be born, and He already knows the day I'll get to hug Him for real. Between those two dates, the right-now moments, I want to make sure I live the life He died on the cross for me to live. I want to give love and grace to those around me and give myself grace when I fail to do so well.

The clock hits 5:22 twice a day. Sometimes I see it twice, other days just once, most days I don't see it at all, but when I do, I treasure the moment, smile, and receive the hug God is giving me.

Lord, thank you for our "such a time as this" reminders. Reminders that you love us. Thank you that anything we walk through from our birth date to our death date, we are not alone.

Amen!

TODAY'S TREASURES

DAY 6

I couldn't stop thanking God for you - every time I prayed, I'd think of you and give thanks. But I do more than thank. I ask - ask the God of our Master, Jesus Christ, the God of glory - to make you intelligent and discerning in knowing him personally, your eyes focused and clear, so that you can see exactly what it is he is calling you to do, grasp the immensity of this glorious way of life he has for Christians, oh, the utter extravagance of his work in us who trust him - endless energy, boundless strength!

EPHESIANS 1:16-19 (THE MESSAGE)

GROWN

Several weeks before our oldest, Ian, was about to graduate high school, I found myself mourning the loss of him like he was about to be gone forever. He was only preparing for a total life change – headed to college an hour and half away. Okay, okay, total life change for me. Complete excitement for him.

I just couldn't wrap my head around the fact that it was here. When he was 18 months old, I just knew those days of diapers, sippy cups, and security blankets would last forever. Yet here we were 18 years later, and it came like a thief in the night and turned my baby into a man.

Fast forward past moving him into the dorm his freshman year, moving him out as summer approached, now pause with me has we take in the moment of moving him into his apartment to begin his sophomore year. He was ready to go. Any growth that was meant to be done in our home was over and it was so evident – he wouldn't be coming home as often. He had established himself so well, made good connections, and carried a confidence I admired.

When we left him that afternoon, I didn't find myself walking away with sadness. Instead, I treasured the moment of getting to walk away knowing he was good. He loves being there and that brings me peace – like being doused with the oil of joy instead mourning. It was an amazing realization that our family isn't growing apart but growing stronger.

Now instead of praying out of fear because I didn't what it was going to be like sending a child off to college, I can pray the verse from Ephesians over Ian and give God all the thanks for the excitement of Ian's future!

Lord, thank you that you hear our prays both chaotic and calm. I pray Your voice be bigger in the lives of our children than any voice in the world. You love our babies more than we do, so, we can trust them in Your hands to protect them and guide them. Therefore, we ask, make them intelligent and discerning in knowing You personally, their eyes focused and clear, so that they can see exactly what it is You are calling them to do.
Amen!

TODAY'S TREASURES

DAY 7

May the Lord bless you and protect you; may the Lord make his face shine on you and be gracious to you; may the Lord look with favor on you and give you peace.

NUMBERS 6:24-26 (CSB)

SWEET SATURDAY

I love Saturday mornings. They are my absolute favorite. We sleep in a little longer. Eric and I make a big breakfast together. Since we're talking about favorite things, breakfast is my absolute favorite food. Bacon, eggs, biscuits and gravy – get in my belly! I also love Saturdays because the slow pace of the morning allows for extra Jesus time. I read every morning of the week, but Saturday mornings are unrushed and uninterrupted. I've become good at saying no to a lot of things that would take away from my Saturday morning time – I just treasure it too much to give it away easily. This isn't because I'm lazy or unsocial. I need this time so I can be better for the things that do get a yes.

There's a chair in our bedroom, it's where I read my Bible and journal. It's where I linger a little longer on Saturday mornings. There's always a moment where I just sit with my eyes closed and smile because I can sense the Lord's face shining on me. Not because of who I am or anything I've done. There's no performance. No proving. It's just He and I delighting in each other, and it brings me such peace. He is such a blessing to me.

Of course, this is a time I've grown into as our boys have grown older. With every season, finding this treasured time with Jesus will look different. Don't feel guilty for allowing yourself to take time for moments with Him. It's the best example you can set for little (or big) eyes that may be watching. Yes, showing them that time alone with Jesus is important but it's also important to show them it's okay to be still and embrace the quiet of a Saturday morning.

Thank you, Jesus, for the peace you provide in the still and for the blessing that saying "no" is okay.
Amen!

TODAY'S TREASURES

DAY 8

It is more blessed [and brings greater joy] to give than to receive.

ACTS 20:35 (AMP)

THE GIFT OF GIVING

I love giving gifts to people. It's one of my favorite things to do—worship being my #1 favorite thing. In any conversation with someone, I'll store away little details they've shared and that becomes my shopping list. I want to make people feel special, making them feel heard and seen. By doing this, my eyes and ears are on others, not myself.

Gifting is a noise stopper for me.

You see, some days I just get all in my head. It gets all noisy in there with overthinking every scenario of life. One particular day I woke up not feeling very special, because I had been overthinking everything. To cope with this, I know that when my thoughts automatically start focusing on myself, it's time to give someone a gift. This gets my mind focused on others. It quiets the noise in my head and turns my overthinking into thoughtfulness. It truly brings me joy, too. It was a treasured moment one day when I gave a small token of thoughtfulness to an unexpected friend. My heart was full, and I saw her face was full-on smile mode.

This is what Jesus did for us when he gave himself on the cross. His eyes were on us, not himself, so we could receive the gift of forgiveness. May His example work its way through all of us.

*Lord, thank you for leading us so well in the gift of giving. May our hearts always be open to being outward focused – lifting others above ourselves.
Amen!*

TODAY'S TREASURES

DAY 9

Then he went down to Nazareth with them and was obedient to them. But his mother treasured all these things in her heart.

LUKE 2:51 (CSB)

SUPER UBER

Right before this verse in Luke, we learn that Jesus' mom and dad started a journey home from Jerusalem, assuming that Jesus was with them. Yet, the whole time, Jesus had stayed behind to teach at "his Father's house," the temple. They didn't have Life 360 back then, so I'm giving Mary a free pass on the mom guilt. It took three days for them to be reunited. Can you even imagine the emotions she went through as a mom?

Here's the main thing I notice: she may have had some emotions, but she didn't get angry when she found Jesus teaching His elders in the temple. No, it says she treasured these things in her heart.

This verse has reminded me that even my frustrations should be treasured. There was a time that I was completely fed-up with my middle son, Isaiah. He was 15 years old, and I felt like I was his personal Uber more than I was his mother, driving him here, there, and everywhere to be with his friends. He loves his friends and I love that he is social, but I was getting overwhelmed by always having to check up on his plans and knowing where he was going to be headed next. So, after reading this scripture, I decided to start treasuring the moments in the car with him. Instead of freaking out and asking "Why do I always have to take you somewhere?" I decided to treasure the small talk we'll make on the way. I treasured the time I got to spend with him, even if it was a car ride. I treasured the good friends that surround him. And I trusted that the prayers I have prayed for him would allow me to see the treasures God has in store for his future.

He is now driving on his own and that comes with a whole new level of independence that I'm learning to treasure.

Lord, thank for lessons that teach to recognize the miraculous in the mundane. When our hope is in you and not in our plans, our expectations, or our performance than finding the treasure in the daily interruptions will be easier. Amen!

TODAY'S TREASURES

DAY 10

Jesus said to them, "Come and have breakfast."

JOHN 21:12 (CSB)

THE TABLE

When our were boys young, having the whole family around the table at supper time was a staple of our weekly routine. Now that the boys have grown up, all of us being together at supper time is few and far between. Especially with our oldest away at college. I still request it of the other two at least twice a week.

After a full day at work, I long to be with my family. Don't get me wrong, I love my work-family, but I get to see them eight hours a day, Monday through Friday. So, sometimes it feels like I see them more than my real family, as if there are deep gaps throughout my day. It's why sitting around the table with Eric and our boys fills my heart.

I think Jesus knew it's good for us to be gathered for a meal. After a long night of fishing, He invites the disciples to breakfast where they have really good conversation. He knew they were missing Him, so He sits with them. Jesus always had a great sense of "withness." You know, being a witness to people by being with them. Though He often withdrew to pray, He knew it was important to be with others. To listen to them. To laugh with them. To pray with them.

I don't know a better place to display "withness" than at the table. Whether it is with your family, or friends, take a seat. Enjoy their company. Laugh with them and love them. Just remember, it's your withness that makes the memories grateful.

Lord, you will never leave us nor forsake us. Thank you for being with us when we gather. Help us to be aware when things are getting too busy so we can make time to be around the table.
Amen!

TODAY'S TREASURES

DAY 11

In God, whose word I praise, in God I trust; I will not be afraid. What can mere mortals do to me?

PSALMS 56:4 (CSB)

HOLD YOUR TORCH HIGH

Holding onto a dream is like holding a torch. Picture the Statue of Liberty, boldly holding a dream up high. A dream is like a torch in that it enlightens a pathway to discover something new up ahead. I hold that torch up high when it comes to my dreams because the higher I hold it, the more I can see what it takes for my dreams to come to life. Of course, it makes me excited and proud to hold that torch up high! There have been times in my excitement that I've shared a dream with others, like passing on my torch for them to hold and see for themselves what I'm dreaming. But rather than hold the torch high, they just put the torch down and the flame quickly fades. It just didn't seem to spark their enthusiasm the same as it sparked mine.

The act of sharing my dream with others has become personal for me. To protect my torch from being snuffed out, I've learned that I don't want to share my dream with just anyone.

With that being said, I had a dream of writing this book of devotions. I was a little apprehensive when I felt God telling me to share my dream to a friend. I feared that even my trusted friend may not be enlightened the way I was. I questioned God. "Are you sure this shouldn't just stay between me and you, God? I'm pretty sure You or Eric are the only ones I can trust with my dreams, right?" But deep down, I felt like God wanted me to trust in Him, not the hands that I shared it with.

A few weeks later—yes, it took me a few weeks to work up the nerves to share—I confided in her. I passed my torch into her hands, and she held it up high. She celebrated with me the dream I shared with her. I left the moment thanking God, for I trusted in Him rather than the fear of what others might think. Seeking first His plan and trusting Him to provide what comes of it.

Never be afraid to dream. Even if others don't understand your dream, you don't have to share it with everyone (unless God tells you to). No matter what, keep holding it up high and walk the path God has prepared for you.

He may challenge us to do things we aren't comfortable doing. He does this to teach us what faithfulness truly means. The Bible says He is a lamp unto our feet. When we dream according to His plans, He will light up our path. Even more reason to hold our torch up high!

Lord, thank you being the faithful Father that you are. You already know all my hopes and dreams. Yet, when I give them to you in prayer you always handle them with care. Amen!

TODAY'S TREASURES

DAY 12

This is the confidence we have before him: If we ask anything according to his will, he hears us.

1 JOHN 5:14 (CSB)

SAY IT

When no one else knows what they want to eat, he knows, and he says it. When no one else knows what they want to do, he knows, and he says it. When no one else knows what they are looking for, he knows, and he says it. He even knows what he doesn't want, and he says it.

I noticed this one day as me and Eric were knocking the words around, "I don't know. What do you want?" Like we were in the middle of a game of ping pong. Back and forth. We were making a simple decision of choosing a place to eat even more complicated than it should be. Then, our oldest son, Ian, walked into the room. Our indecisive ping pong was suddenly cut short because he knew what he wanted. And that's where we went. I treasured his confidence and his ability to say what he wanted when it was needed.

Ian also knows when he can come to us in confidence to ask for something. If it's in our power or in the realm of our approval, we will make it happen. He has never been afraid to ask. I've learned a lot from his assured practice when it comes to my own assurance in asking. I've often assumed what I'm asking for is beyond God's scope of importance, or that I don't deserve it.

God is a loving and generous God. Like a parent, maybe He's waiting on the ask. Maybe He's waiting on us to make up our mind. Rather than going back and forth, playing ping pong about a decision, let's decide with confidence.

Lord, thank you that we can come to you and know in confidence that you hear us. I pray we would always seek your will above our own because your will is good and perfect.
Amen!

TODAY'S TREASURES

DAY 13

That's why I don't think there's any comparison between the present hard times and the coming good times. The created world itself can hardly wait for what's coming next. Everything in creation is being more or less held back. God reins it in until both creation and all the creatures are ready and can be released at the same moment into the glorious times ahead. Meanwhile, the joyful anticipation deepens.

ROMANS 8:19-21 (THE MESSAGE)

JOYFUL ANTICIPATION

I love the feeling of excitement. I love knowing that something good is coming. It's why I've always loved the Christmas season, birthdays, vacation, or any holiday that's a day off work – exciting!

If you would ever ask me to pray for you, I will pray with honor. With much anticipation, I'll exclaim, "It's like waiting for Christmas!" Because waiting to see what God will do with our prayers is so exciting to me. He may not send the answered prayer wrapped in an ornamented package, but it doesn't mean that something great isn't coming. The people of Israel didn't expect the Messiah to be a baby wrapped in a manger. God always knows best!

One day not too long ago, I was communicating in a group text. Group texts aren't always my favorite, but we were hosting a dinner at our home. I was giving details of the evening, trying to convey my anticipation of the awesomeness that was sure to greet everyone once we were all together. However, I don't think my excitement translated well through a text message, because everyone received my anticipation by responding with "haha" popups to my message.

Unfortunately, the term anticipation doesn't always get received with joy. Sometimes it nestles its way into a person causing doubt, fear, and anxiety. The group probably thought I was being sarcastically funny; there's no way she could be excited to host. But I really was excited! Not everything has to be dreaded. I'd prefer joyful anticipation. I went to bed that night treasuring my excitement.

Lord, thank you that because of Jesus we look forward with hope to the good times and the bad. Because you work all things together for the good and nothing compares to the joy that is coming.
Amen!

TODAY'S TREASURES

DAY 14

My grace is sufficient for you, for my power is perfected in weakness.

2 CORINTHIANS 12:9 (CSB)

IMPERFECTIONS

My Isaiah (our middle son) is artsy like his daddy. He can draw, paint, design on the computer, he even has an eye for fashion. I have several pieces of his artwork hanging or sitting around our home. He doesn't really like that I use his work as decoration because all he sees are the imperfections. Don't we assume that's all others will see? But I love everything about what his hands have made. From the lopsided bowl he made sitting on out coffee table, to the pencil sketch drawing of two deer hanging on the wall, I treasure them because I love him.

Penciled right into 2 Corinthians 12, Paul talks about how he pleaded with the Lord 3 times to take away his imperfection (the thorn in his flesh). God's response: "My grace is sufficient for you, for my power is perfected in weakness." Grace, then, is God favoring us with his presence, love, help, and power. Our imperfections are opportunities for us to depend on God's grace to accomplish his purposes. Maybe they're a humble reminder that this life isn't all about us. It's about bringing glory to the creator, not the creation. I think Paul had figured this out when he said, "That is why, for Christs sake, I delight in weaknesses, in insults, in hardships, in persecutions, in difficulties. For when I am weak, then I am strong." He knew this life on earth, while progressive, is not complete until we are face-to-face with Jesus.

God doesn't only the imperfections of His masterpieces. He sees his beloved. Every time we are face-to-face with ourselves in a mirror, or when Isaiah walks past one of his pieces of art our eyes may be drawn to our imperfections, but when we look to Him, we are radiant, and our faces shall never be ashamed (Psalm 34:5).

Lord, I pray for eyes to see the way you see. That we would see beauty in our scars, loveliness in our flaws, and goodness in our lack because that's where You shine the brightest.
Amen!

TODAY'S TREASURES

DAY 15

Finally, brothers and sisters, whatever is true, whatever is honorable, whatever is just, whatever is pure, whatever is lovely, whatever is commendable—if there is any moral excellence and if there is anything praiseworthy—dwell on these things.

PHILIPPIANS 4:8 (CSB)

GOOD MASCARA DAY

Mascara. Some days, it just goes everywhere but where I want it to go. I guess there are mornings when my right hand has a mind of its own. So, when it has control of my mascara wand, the black lengthening formula can end up smudged across my temple, dotting the side of my nose, or found speckled all over my eyelid. It can be super frustrating, yet it doesn't have to alter my whole day.

Putting on mascara takes a maximum of 5 minutes out of my day, so to let it have control of a full 24-hour day would be foolish. Still, there's been times I've let a small mascara frustration bring me down. Why? Because I'm looking for everything to be perfect, everything to go how I want it to go, and everything to align just right. In my human brain that's where I'll find peace.

The Apostle Paul, in Philippians 4:8, turns our gaze in another direction though, giving us a new perspective. Paul says focus on what's true. Truth is perfect. Paul says take part in what's honorable. There's nothing honorable about wanting everything to go your way. He says to dwell on what's commendable, excellent, and praiseworthy. When we find ourselves still seeking the good, beyond the frustration, that's something to be admired.

The morning I wrote this could have easily been described as a bad mascara day, but I renamed it a good mascara day. I pulled those sticky eyelashes apart and simply moved on. I treasured that moment, as hard as it was! I dare say, remarkably, I've also had good mascara days too! You know, the days when it goes on just right. When we find good in the bad days, it makes the good days even greater. I will proudly exclaim, "That's the way to start a day!"

Lord, I pray for the strength to rename every moment that comes to steal, kill, and destroy my day. I have the power of the resurrected King living on the inside of me – I can turn a bad moment into a great day.
Amen!

TODAY'S TREASURES

DAY 16

Sing a new song to him; play skillfully on the strings, with a joyful shout.

PSALMS 33:3 (CSB)

DON'T WASTE THE MOMENT

By: Ian Bivens

For most of my life, my free time was spent playing basketball and video games. Every day was a routine: go to school, go to basketball practice, then come home and play video games. In between all of that, I would get homework done and mow the yard too.

In the middle of my junior year of high school, life took a turn. Our family moved from West Virginia to Kentucky. My first goal: join the school basketball team. Yet, being the new kid, basketball just didn't feel the same as it used to. Not long after moving, schools closed due to the pandemic, and I was stuck at home playing video games all day. Our new house didn't even have a driveway to play basketball on. I was getting bored and video games weren't cutting it.

One day I was listening to the radio and heard a song by Lynyrd Skynyrd, so I picked up my dad's guitar and tried to play it. At seventeen years of age, I had never played a guitar before. I was so intrigued by the sounds that I found myself watching beginner videos on YouTube and asking my dad questions.

This curiosity to play changed my life and before I knew it, I was playing guitar more than basketball or video games. Over the last three years I have gotten much better and have even played on stage numerous times. Looking back, I'm grateful I learned something new because I discovered something I never knew I had within me.

I feel like that's a lesson so many of us could learn, not wasting a moment. Just as I used the boring moments during covid to learn something new, it grew into a passion. Is there something you want to learn? Something you've never tried before?

Don't waste the moment. Just start! You'll be glad you did.

Lord, thank you for allowing us the time we need to find the treasures you've buried inside of us. You've equipped us with everything we need for your purposes. Give us eyes to see and ears to hear all that you have for us – don't let us waste a moment.
Amen!

TODAY'S TREASURES

DAY 17

> *Now if by grace, then it is not by works; otherwise, grace ceases to be grace.*
>
> ROMANS 11:6 (CSB)

SELF-GRACE

Everybody makes mistakes. Nobody's perfect. We've all been told those words and they are good words to live by. Even so, it's difficult to let them penetrate our hearts and minds at times. I'm really good at beating myself up and really bad at giving myself grace. If I mess up, it's like the end of the world. At work, I keep a printed quote close to my eyes that reminds me, "There has never been a day when God has panicked and thought…she's ruined everything." This quote makes me giggle, yet it's so true.

For this reason, the day I noticed I had actually given myself grace I took note and treasured it in my heart. It was a big deal to me. No one else may have noticed it but I knew it was a growth step for myself. I've written several blogs on my website, Freeandfancy.com, about learning to be FREE from the false feelings of lack, limitations, and lies. Why not find some humor in our growth? Why not take confidence in ourselves, so we can start living our style of FANCY, the way God created us to live? I mean every word of the statement, to be free and fancy. That day, when I found humor in my mistake and allowed myself to learn from it instead of beating myself up, it was very freeing.

Why do I assume I have the power to completely ruin everything anyway? If I don't have the power to ruin everything, then I also don't have the power to beat myself up for it. Let's stop giving ourselves credit for all the bad and start giving ourselves more grace.

Lord, thank you that my daily portion of grace isn't based on performance or perfection. You give it freely before I've done anything. That's what grace is – undeserved blessing. May I continue to learn from your example, giving out grace to those around me and to myself.
Amen!

TODAY'S TREASURES

DAY 18

I am able to do all things through him who strengthens me.

PHILIPPIANS 4:13 (CSB)

MY SWISS ARMY KNIFE

Honey, can you fix this? Babe, can you hang that? Sweetness, would you jump out of an airplane? Eric, will you pray for me? Of course, to me, my husband is all-that-and-a-can-of-Pringles. Others have described him as a Swiss Army Knife. This is because he can literally do anything.

Is he perfect at everything? No. Is everything fixed with one trip to Lowes? No. Does he sometimes hang a frame too high on the wall when I wanted the frame to be a little lower to my eye? Yes. So, if he's not perfect, what is it that makes him known as a Swiss Army Knife? Easy answer: he is not afraid to try. If he gets it wrong the first time, he tries again. If he doesn't know the answer, he Googles it. He searches for the solution, or he figures out a way to get it done with what he's got.

Although a Swiss Army Knife is known to be a multi-use tool that can be valuable for any adventure, it is nothing unless someone holds it and uses it. We all have gifts and abilities. Some of us, like Eric, aren't afraid to use them. Others may be leaving our Swiss Army Knife sitting in the junk drawer. But your gifts and abilities are not meant to sit in a drawer. They are meant to be used.

I want to become a tool of multi-use goodness. I want to try new things. I want to be ready for any adventure.

Lord, sometimes the greatest things are considered the smallest in the world's eyes. Help us not to lose sight of what's important. In our striving to accomplish, may we know all our strength comes from you.
Amen!

TODAY'S TREASURES

DAY 19

The Lord answered her, "Martha, Martha, you are worried and upset about many things, but one thing is necessary. Mary has made the right choice, and it will not be taken away from her."

ROMANS 11:6 (CSB)

FULFILLMENT IN A GOOD NO

I did it! I said, "No!"

I couldn't believe it but that little two letter word brought me a sense of freedom as it nervously tumbled out of my mouth. I mean, yes, I could meet for dinner with another friend. Yes, I could be out for the third time that week. Yes, I could fit in one more meeting, and yes, I could have fun doing it all. But saying yes will also drain me mentally and physically, along with taking away my quality time with family.

It's time to figure out there's power in a good no, so we can say a good yes. Our identity isn't found in busy. There's no true fulfillment in a full schedule. We live a full life out of the strength God has given us, not the strength we think we have in ourselves. Not by might, nor by power, but by My spirit, says the Lord. We fear missing out, not moving up, not being enough if we're not involved or a part of everything, but that spirit of missing out does not come from God. It comes from self.

Notice in the scripture for today that Mary said no to many things and yes to Jesus. What if we practiced that? Sitting with Jesus first. Then maybe we wouldn't be worried and upset like Martha because we've filled ourselves with The One Thing first. When we are focused on Him, we are planning our schedules to spend time with Him and protecting ourselves from being too busy.

Lord, you are the one true thing that brings fulfillment. May we lay our lives down, becoming a little lighter and giving ourselves room to pick up new life in you.
Amen!

TODAY'S TREASURES

DAY 20

Weeping may endure for the night, but joy comes in the morning.

PSALMS 30:5 (AMPC)

MORNING HUMS

It was Sunday night. The next day, the start of a brand-new school year. He didn't want to go to bed. Nope, instead, he hem-hawed around. He delayed the inevitable as long as he possibly could. He performed a quick comedy routine. He even tried to get in a wrestling match with dad (dad will always wrestle). Eventually, we prayed, and Eli went to bed.

Eli may be difficult at times to get to bed but when it comes to waking up, he is the easiest kid to wake up. I walk in his room, turn off his fan, lean over his sweet, slumbering self and whisper "good morning angel face." He'll give a little moan letting me know he hears me and giving me permission to please exit the premises.

Before I'm even back in my bathroom I can hear him moving around. That particular morning, the first day of school, I heard the most joyful sound. Eli was humming. This is not an unusual occurrence for Eli. If he's not talking, he can often be heard humming or singing. However, since he had found it such a bummer to go to bed the night before, I found it comforting to hear him displaying joy in the morning.

I find Eli's singing and humming a symptom of joy or happiness, especially when he does it unknowingly. He is naturally joyful. He didn't have to have a reason for it. He still had to go to school. He just discovered a way to consider it pure joy when faced with troubles of many kinds. For a middle schooler, school can be a terrible trouble.

Lord, no matter what may lay before us, let the joy we find in you be our strength. I pray that strength finds us praising you, the One where our help comes from, the maker of heaven and earth.
Amen!

TODAY'S TREASURES

DAY 21

Give thanks in everything; for this is God's will for you in Christ Jesus.

1 THESSALONIANS 5:18 (CSB)

JUST SAY, "THANK YOU"

Them: "Jodie, I love your outfit today!"

Me: "It's old and I just something I threw on."

If there's anyone in the world who is learning how to receive a compliment correctly, it's me. There have been times when people have given me kind words and I'll return their kindness with a reason for how I could've done better. I'll point out something negative about myself to balance out their positive sentiment. It's as if I feel the need to explain that the shirt is old and has a microscopic sized hole in the armpit.

Why do I feel the need to swat at their compliment like it's a pesky fly? Because I don't think I deserve them? I've noticed that once the words hit my ears, my mind finds it easier to explain the flaws, rather than just say, "Thank you" and receive the kindness.

Paul advises us in 1 Thessalonians to give thanks in everything. Notice it doesn't say give thanks "for" everything, but instead, "in" everything. Give thanks when someone notices something in you. Even if the compliment is for the clothes you are wearing, your choice of style came from your inner most thoughts, so receive the compliment. Give thanks when someone sees the perfect in your imperfection. They aren't expecting you to live up to perfection for them, but simply recognizing that you make the good stand out to them.

So, I'm learning to just say "Thank you" with grace and elegance. No explanation. Just simply giving others the gift of receiving their words and not swatting them away but treasuring them.

Lord, I pray for the one who is having a hard time today and just can't see the good, that you would open her heart and mind to receive an encouraging word today. May it be so obviously you, that the only words she can muster are, "thank you."
Amen!

TODAY'S TREASURES

_____

_____

_____

_____

_____

_____

_____

_____

_____

_____

_____

_____

_____

_____

DAY 22

Brothers do not be children in your thinking. Be infants in evil, but in your thinking be mature.

1 CORINTHIANS 14:20 (ESV)

MATURING UP

Every day throughout an entire year, I wrote in my "Tiny Treasures" journal. Now, looking through it, I find an entry that says, "I switched perspectives and I got over something today." I didn't give detail on the something that I got over, but that's okay. The point is, I've learned there are some things that are not worth allowing to take over me. Instead, I can take over some things by switching the way I see them.

I can choose to take captive any thought, frustration, or situation. Rather than allowing my thinking to be immature, I can switch perspectives and consider how thinking maturely will lead to a better outcome. We all have days when it's just hard to think maturely. Some days it's easier to snap at someone than to consider understanding them. Days when it's faster to just do it ourselves because teaching someone to learn takes too much patience in the moment. Days when it's easier to curl up on the couch with your blanket then go out and connect with people.

When you choose the perspective that brings honor to others and glory to God, then you know you're not only growing up, you're maturing up.

Lord, you are where our help comes from. You are our refuge and our strength. When it's easier to look inward, may your Holy Spirit remind us we have the power to choose mature. Amen!

TODAY'S TREASURES

DAY 23

Many plans are in a person's heart, but it is the Lord's purpose that prevails.

PROVERBS 19:21 (CSB)

DIVINE INTERVENING

The supper plans were set, and they had been since Friday night. That's when I do the grocery order and plan the next week's meals. Thursday night we'll grill hamburgers. I like to know ahead of time so I can get my taste buds ready, and they were ready for burgers that night.

Throughout the day, however, it started coming to my attention that our two boys were making other plans for themselves. Good plans, they just didn't match my plans. One was going in this direction for the evening and the other needed our parental-taxi services to make his plans happen. Of course, we obliged and in a matter of minutes it was just Eric and me who would be having dinner, no kiddos. A decision had to be made. Do we still want to make burgers just for us?

Even though we had recently gone on a date night, another date night couldn't hurt, right? We said no to burgers and yes to going out. Arriving at our chosen destination, we were quickly seated, and we ordered the usual. But then something else happened, not really unusual, just unplanned. I started a conversation I really needed to have. I just didn't realize it would be right then. Yet isn't that how God orchestrates His most beautiful plans? What may feel like a surprise to us may be part of His providence all along. He knew I needed to get all those thoughts out of my head and into the wise ears of my husband. God knew I couldn't have got it out at the dinner table with my boys around; He knew I needed audible instruction. Eric was His microphone to me.

Eric listened to me, and then like he always does, he led me. He didn't boss me. He uplifted me and never shamed me. He protected my feelings and never rejected them. He challenged me because he would never let me remain stagnant. My heart needed that release and now my mind could relax.

We often think obvious peace follows a well-planned schedule, but in God's divine intervening, we find His plans prevail.

Lord, give us eyes to see the interruptions in our day as God moments for something better. Being slow to frustration, but quick in gratitude.
Amen!

TODAY'S TREASURES

DAY 24

And he (Azariah) did what was right in the sight of the LORD, according to all that his father Amaziah had done, except that the high places were not removed; the people still sacrificed and burned incense on the high places.

2 KINGS 15:3-4 (CSB)

HEALED HURT

Hi. I'm Jodie and I've been hurt.

Honestly, I think there is something relieving about saying that out loud. It's a recognition of, "Hey, this is real and needs healing."

But before I had come to a place of saying it out loud, the hurt had become a "high place" for me. The prophet Jeremiah gives many accounts of high places throughout 1 & 2 Kings. High places were places of worship on elevated pieces of ground, originally dedicated to idol worship.

There were some days I wouldn't think about the hurt at all, but there were other days it was all I would think about. Replaying moments over-and-over in my head, trying to figure out what happened. You could say I was only adding stones to the monument of hurt, because I never really removed the high place.

I had to stop trying to make sense of it in my own understanding and trust the Lord to make my paths straight. And He did. He has shown me how beauty has come from the ashes. I just couldn't see the beauty because the high places were blocking everything.

People aren't perfect, so hurtful things will always be something we have to walk through in all areas of life. Regardless, it's up to us to address those situations sooner than not at all. No matter what, God can still work in the midst of hurt. A greater story can still be told. For me, I now consider it growing pains in preparation for greater things to come.

Despite the healing that has relieved the hurt, there are still times when I'll feel a sting from the past. There are times when it is easy to compare the past to the present. No one who surrounds my present deserves that comparison. So, I'm learning (always learning) to pick up the rubble left over from the high places and throw them away, humbly letting go of the hurt. Choosing humility over hurt. It's not about me. It's not how it made me feel. It's not even the hurt itself. It's about God's providence and how He continues to use my story for His good. I didn't think I would ever say I treasure a season of hurt, but I've seen God's light shine bright through the broken places.

I bow to Him, not the hurt. He is my high place.

Lord, thank you for the broken places that lead to healed spaces. You will use every story on our timeline for our good and your glory. I pray I am always here for it – here I am Lord, use me.
Amen!

TODAY'S TREASURES

DAY 25

From the rising of the sun to its setting, let the name of the Lord be praised.

PSALMS 113:3 (CSB)

SUNRISE & SUNSET

The rising and setting of the sun can paint the most beautiful masterpieces in the sky. The reds, oranges, purples, and pinks that cover the distant landscape is breathtaking. My husband smiles at me because I'm often taking pictures of pretty sunrises or sunsets; my phone is full of pictures of the sky. Yet, as beautiful as the scenes were to my eyes when viewing the sky in person, the pictures don't fully measure up to the in-person view. The sun appears so much smaller when viewed on a phone.

The morning and evening sky is such a treasure to me because it demonstrates God's creativity in creation. He didn't just splatter-paint everything into existence. He put great thought and care into every decision. The result: His creation is great.

Genesis 1:16 mentions the greater light that rules over the day, which we call the sun. The rising of the sun is the start of something new. A brand-new day we get to experience. In the day-to-day experiences, we can work through challenges that make us stronger. We can celebrate wins with our friends. The setting of the sun is an opportunity to leave the day's worries where they were formed. We can thank God for that day's portion of grace and strength. We can rest in His goodness. He gives us exactly what we need for each day.

Even though the sun is large, bright, and needed every day, it's easy to overlook its faithfulness. Yet, even on a cloudy day, when we can't see or feel the goodness of the sun, it's still rising and setting, and it's still shining. How awesome is our Creator!

Lord, thank you for creation. I pray with the rising and setting of today's sun that we would bring you praise allowing the worries of the day to be seen as small compared the greatness of the Son.
Amen!

TODAY'S TREASURES

DAY 26

If a ruler's anger rises against you, do not leave your post; calmness can lay great offenses to rest.

ECCLESIASTES 10:4 (CSB)

ROYALTY IN LOYALTY

By: Eli Bivens

As a teenage boy, making your dad proud is pretty much your entire goal in life. Sports is a good example. Me and my dad play tennis together. Now, I know what you're thinking "a 43-year-old man playing tennis?" Yeah, I know right, he's old! But he sometimes still beats my butt and I get really mad. As a dad, he doesn't care if I mess up or play bad. He just doesn't want me to get mad, lose my focus, and quit. Instead, he encourages me and challenges me to get better.

Same thing with God. He doesn't care how good or how imperfect you are. He just wants us to stay loyal to his word, and not get angry, lose focus, or quit on him. Ecclesiastes 10:4 says, "If a ruler's anger rises against you, do not leave your post; calmness can lay great offenses to rest." In a tough moment, sometimes all you want to do is get revenge or let out your anger, but what you should do is keep your calm and you will be rewarded.

Lord, thank you for what you have already done and will continue to do through me. I pray that you will remind me how perfect you are and how much you can do. Make me aware that you will always love me and will never look at me different because of what I do.
Amen!

TODAY'S TREASURES

DAY 27

Do not be misled: Bad company corrupts good character.

1 CORINTHIANS 15:33 (NIV)

GOOD COMPANY

Throughout our marriage, Eric has told me several memories of his time spent with his church's youth group. From the life-changing worship services that led them deeper into a relationship with Jesus, to the silly acts of tee-peeing the homes of their youth group leaders. Even his sister, Misty, has shared some memorable stories, one of which is about her and her friends singing the song, "I Would Walk 500 Miles." Now, anytime I hear that song I think of that story and it's not even my memory.

I've always wished for youth group stories of my own but my memories from a youth group are limited. I was 20 years old when I went to my first youth group service, yet it's the best memory because that's where I fully gave my heart to The Lord. With Eric's many memories and mine combined, I prayed countless prayers for our boys to have youth group memories of their own.

God heard those prayers and allowed our boys to have some amazing leaders take them under their wings and guide them in building good character, in ways a parent alone can't always achieve. You know the saying, "It takes a village." I am grateful for the youth leaders who have become a part of our village. Not only have youth leaders been a blessing, but our boys have made great friends in youth group, too. They've had the privilege of being surrounded by some of the best friends a mom could ask for, helping them create memories that will last 500 miles.

My favorite memories of the boys in youth group are the days they come home from camp. Every year, they come back exhausted, yet so ready to pour out their "I Would Walk 500 Miles" stories. I treasure every single one like it was my own.

Lord, thank you that you hear a momma's prayer. I know our kids will never be perfect, mistakes will be made, but I'm so thankful for the foundation that keeps them steady when the world comes to shake it. Keep them surrounded by good company all the days of their life.
Amen!

TODAY'S TREASURES

DAY 28

Be strong and do the work.

1 CHRONICLES 28:10 (CSB)

TEMPLES AND THRONES

While doing my devotion one morning, nothing spectacular seemed to pop out at me from what I was reading. Sometimes I feel like I'm just reading to get through it. What I've come to realize is that God still uses those "get through it" moments for a lesson a little bit later. He doesn't waste anything.

It wasn't until that afternoon, while I was cleaning toilets, I started thinking, "Is this really the most important thing I have to do today, really?" At that time, while I was kneeling over a toilet bowl, God decided to highlight my "get through it" moment from that morning.

I had been reading in 1 Chronicles 28. David is encouraging Solomon to pursue a real relationship with God, to serve Him, and to build the temple for the Lord. Solomon was building and I was cleaning, neither one of us felt fully committed in the moment but David exhorts to Solomon, and to us, be strong and do the work. He tells him twice, in 1 Chronicles 28:20 we find David again spurring Solomon on, "Be strong and courageous, and do the work. Do not be afraid or discouraged, for the Lord God, my God, is with you. He will not fail you or forsake you until all the work for the service of the temple of the Lord is finished".

Temples and thrones, they're the same, right? So, I had this to decide: I could allow the moment to steal my joy, or I could allow it to build my joy. I chose the latter. God sees my faithfulness to my family, and I trust that even when I'm just getting through it, He is using it for a purpose.

Lord, thank you that you don't waste the mundane moments of our day. When we are willing, you are faithful. Amen!

TODAY'S TREASURES

DAY 29

Trust in the Lord with all your heart, and do not rely on your own understanding; in all your ways know him, and he will make your paths straight.

PROVERBS 3:5-6 (CSB)

REDISPLAY

One step away. Have you ever been just one step away from success? One move away from victory? One try away from getting it right?

There was one, simple task on the computer that I had been shown how to do several times. I had practiced this task with veterans of the job. I had notes. For real, I have a whole 3-ring binder titled, "Jodie's In-A-Bind Binder" full of notes on how to do my job right.

Then it came time for me to do the task on my own. At each attempt, I would get to the point where it didn't look like it did when others would perform the task. So, I would stop and go get help every time. Unsure of the next steps, it felt as if I was not capable of learning how to do it on my own. I uttered the words, "I guess you really can't teach an old dog new tricks."

During one of my run-and-get-help instances, a supervisor offered to walk me through it again step-by-step. She recognized my assumption that I was doing it wrong, and she said, "You're not doing it wrong. You just need to click redisplay at this point." When I hit redisplay, the screen changed, and it all came together like it was supposed to! My notes were spot on. I did each step according to what I was taught, but one simple word—one single step—was missing: redisplay. Mind blown, I excitedly exclaimed,

"Sugar and spice, are you kidding me? That's it? That's what was keeping me from finishing?"

Are you one step away from completing that application you've been putting off? You could be one more, get-back-up away from landing that back handspring. One try away from not being rejected this time. One look away from finding the perfect house. One yes away from the perfect opportunity. One prayer away from healing. You're not too old. You're not too young. You're not too far behind. You're not too busy. Click redisplay on your mindset. This time things could all come together.

What if Abraham and Sarah simply didn't believe God's promise and quit trying to have a baby? What if Esther hadn't requested the second dinner party? She and her people may have been killed. What if Samuel hadn't kept interviewing Jesse's sons? What if Mary hadn't kept trying to persuade Jesus to produce more wine at the wedding? He wasn't ready for his ministry of miracles to start but then comes mom clicking redisplay…ministry started. What if Jesus hadn't kept going back to the garden to pray? Thankfully we'll never know. He's a pro at coming back!

Redisplay. Never stop trying. Never stay down.

Lord, you are not a God who gives up. May we follow in your example of perseverance and give it one more prayer. Don't let me stop one step short.
Amen!

TODAY'S TREASURES

DAY 30

Therefore, dear friends, while you wait for these things, make every effort to be found without spot or blemish in his sight, at peace.

2 PETER 3:14 (CSB)

MAKE EVERY EFFORT

Have you ever wanted something so bad you'd do anything to get it? Whether you just had to have it, or you actually needed it. There's no "when in doubt do without" here. Let's just get it already!

Well, our youngest, Eli, experienced this turmoil not too long ago. He asked us every day for this one thing that he wanted so bad. We would explain why we didn't think he needed it. The reason made sense to us as parents. Unfortunately, it never made sense to him.

The same is true for us sometimes when it comes to waiting for our Savior to return. We want Him. We need Him. We don't understand His delay. Nonetheless, Simon Peter motivates us to make every effort to wait while we yearn for our heart's desire. So, we wait patiently with hopeful expectation that all will come to know Christ.

Now, Eli can be a pretty patient kid, unless he is hungry for Mexican, then get the tacos ready 'cause here we come. In this instance, however, he never got upset with our answer. He was just persistent in his pursuit. Then, one evening, while we were sitting on the coach, he came to us carrying a computer in hand. He asks if he can show us something. We obviously said, "Yes." He proceeded by showing us a Power Point presentation that he had put together himself. It was showing the plans and purposes for this thing he wanted. He communicated in very logical and visual detail why it would only make sense for him to get this item. After such a presentation, we gave in and granted his wishes. He had made every effort to not give up. Made every effort to make the most of his wait and I treasured it.

Lord, thank you that you do not delay your promises. You are a promise keeper, and your ways are higher than ours. May we trust you today with the desires of our heart. Amen!

TODAY'S TREASURES

DAY 31

Everyone should look not to his own interests, but rather to the interests of others.

PHILIPPIANS 2:4 (CSB)

BLACK EYES & LITTLE LIES

In a house full of boys, I've been told a few lies. Whether it's not fessing up for who did it, or changing up the facts to alter the truth, I've learned to become an investigator when things look suspicious. There was a time when I was questioning how snacks were disappearing so quickly from the pantry. Nobody fessed up when asked. Ideas were mere distractions from the actual truth. Thanks to home security cameras, we finally discovered that all three boys were sneaking downstairs after mom and dad went to bed so they could get a midnight snack in the kitchen. Like I said, I've learned to become an investigator when things look suspicious.

One morning, I had gone into the boys' rooms to wake them up for school without much thought. They got up as normal, brushed their teeth, then did their normal routine to get ready. I was about to leave for work when I went to give Eli a hug. That's when I noticed a discoloration under his eye. At first, I thought it was just a shadow, but upon further examination it was a black eye!

"Eli! What happened to your eye?"

"Oh, umm, I got up to use the bathroom in the middle of the night and ran into the wall."

"Elijah Pierce, are you telling the truth? One does not get a black eye like that from running into a wall."

"Well, I did."

I let it go for the moment, but I thought about it all day long. My overthinking was reeling with thoughts of teachers turning me in for possible child abuse accusations.

Finally, when we were all home that evening, the investigation started. Finally, the true story came out. Isaiah and Eli had been boxing in Eli's room where Isaiah got in a really good hit to the eye. Eli didn't want his brother to get in trouble, so he made up a little lie to protect both of them. His reasoning, "We were just tussling like brothers do."

Yes, we talked to him about how lying is not okay. Deep down, I loved his heart behind why he did it. I treasured Eli's willingness to put his brother before himself, choosing to see the situation from the point of view that they were in it together. After all, they were just doing what brothers do, and brothers also look out for each other. Whether it's meeting up for a late-night snack or taking the fall for the one who knocked you out. That's brotherly love.

Lord, choosing to love like you can be hard sometimes. I pray for eyes to see from a higher point of view, so I can be a friend who sticks close, like a brother.
Amen!

TODAY'S TREASURES

DAY 32

> Taste and see that the Lord is good. How happy is the person who takes refuge in him!
>
> PSALMS 34:8 (CSB)

HAPPY WITH IT

Early on in ministry, I realized that I wasn't going to be the stereotypical pastor's wife. You know the kind I'm talking about: the domestic goddess of a woman who can cook the best potluck dinner for all guests to taste and see that the food is as good as the Lord. For me, concocting recipes, and the mess that ensues with cooking and cleaning up, will never bring me joy. After many years of trying, I'm completely okay with it now.

There was a time, early on in ministry, when I was trying to be something that I wasn't meant to be. It was at a women's potluck that I finally came to the realization that I'm not meant to be a potluck pastor's wife. I had stressed several days before the event wanting to create a mouth-watering dish that would make everyone talk about how good it was and beg me for the recipe. I craved the attention, but deep down, there was nothing in me that truly desired to create the dish and clean it too. So, what did I take to the potluck that year? A dish that I got from Sam's Club. Was it a hit? Probably not, but the difference was: I got to walk into the gathering toting a real smile, not a fake one covering up stress and the real me. May the undomesticated goddess please stand up!

I can stress to be something that I'm not, or I can take confidence in being who I truly am. God has made each of us differently, for His plans. When I finally realized this, I quit questioning why I wasn't like all the other pastors' wives. He showed me it's not about who I am, but about Who's I was. I can be happy with that.

And by the way, there is now one thing I can cook well. It is potato soup. It's one recipe I can put together with confidence and take to any event proudly. I have tasted and seen that the Lord is good.

Lord, You are good. When things aren't going how we planned – when the ingredients aren't mixing how we had hoped – we can taste and see that You are still good. Amen!

TODAY'S TREASURES

DAY 33

Only goodness and faithful love will pursue me all the days of my life.

PSALMS 23:6 (CSB)

ONE THOUSAND TIMES

One day, when Isaiah was 6 years old, I told him, "I love you." He replied, "I know, you've told me like a thousand times."

Since then, not much has changed with the cutest middle-child you've ever seen. He still rolls his eyes at me when I compliment his handsomeness. He still tries to change the subject when I say, "I love you." I still have to steal hugs, kisses, and sometimes even bribe him for affection. He recently called me "bruh" when I asked for a kiss. But, with the heart of a loving mother, I will pursue him until he leaves this house, because I know one day, he'll cleave to a wife. I love that boy and he will hear me say it every single day I have the chance to say it.

When I think about my pursuit of my boy, despite the heartache it sometimes brings, I can't help but compare it to how God is constantly pursuing us, His children. To Him, we are His chosen ones, His beloved. Despite the heartache we sometimes cause Him, He never ever throws His hands up in defeat. There's a marvelous chunk of verses in Psalm 139 that perfectly describe this great pursuit by our all-knowing, ever-present God. The psalmist writes, where can I go to escape your Spirit? Where can I flee from your presence? If I go to heaven, you are there; if I make my bed in Sheol, you are there. If I live at the eastern horizon or settle at the western limits even there your hand will lead me; your right hand will hold on to me (Psalm 139:7-10).

We can never move beyond God's love or escape His presence. Even if you've only known Him since today, He has known you all of your life. He has always been in pursuit of you, wanting a relationship with you. He loves you so much that He gave His only son for you. Even on a bad day, when it's harder to receive that love, He is there.

There's a worship song by Bethel Music called Goodness of God. A portion of the song goes like this, your goodness is running after, it's running after me. I'm getting teary eyed just typing these words because our God, in His goodness and faithful love, is running after us and will pursue us all the days of our life.

We can make mistakes, be mad at Him, and even call Him "bruh." But being the greatest example of a parent that ever could be, He will tell you I love you a thousand more times!

Treasure His love.

Lord, while we were still sinners you sent your son to die for us. There is and never will be another love like yours. It is unconditional and forgiving. I thank you one thousand times!
Amen!

TODAY'S TREASURES

DAY 34

Then the woman, seeing that she could not go unnoticed, came trembling and fell at his feet.

LUKE 8:47 (NIV)

NOTICED

Some days, I feel like I'm nowhere near the top of the chart when it comes to being a good mom. Some days end with mom apologizing, again. Most of the time, it's because my expectations haven't been met which leads me to frustration.

One morning, I'd had a hard mom morning. Rather than calmly handling the frustration with one of my boys, I just let all frustration out and said way too much. Of course, I recognized it after the fact. And of course, it was a Sunday morning, just before going to church.

By the time I got to church I was holding in tears with big breaths. I wanted to worship unnoticed, so I could cry out to the Lord and let the tears flow. But as I entered the sanctuary, I was spotted by our care pastor. He saw me take one big inhale through my nose and exhale through my mouth. Before he could utter the words, "that was a big breath you just released," waterworks suddenly fell from my eyes. He wrapped me in a caring and friendly hug in that moment, and just let me cry. I told him I just had a hard mom morning. He didn't judge me. He didn't tell me what I could have done better. He simply said, "Jodie, your boys know you love them." With one hug and in six words, I could breathe normally again.

Jesus does the same for the woman in Luke 8. He notices her

in her issue, and with six words she is able to leave healed and in peace. "Daughter, your faith has saved you."

I really wanted to go unnoticed that morning, but God knew I needed a touch in order to move forward in peace. He sees us, He knows us, and He wants good for us.

Lord, you love us too much to let us go unnoticed. Thank you for how you work through people to deliver your message of love.
Amen!

TODAY'S TREASURES

DAY 35

To speak evil of no one, to avoid quarreling, to be gentle, and to show perfect courtesy toward all people.

TITUS 3:2 (ESV)

HE DIDN'T KNOW HOW TO BE MEAN

"Mom, the obituary only said who he was, but it didn't tell anything about WHO he was."

If you've ever had a child lose a classmate, you know it's a gentle process to navigate. During the middle of Eli's eighth grade year, he lost a friend named Emmanuel, who died due to a heart condition. He was from Africa, and not only was he learning American culture, he was also learning how to make friends in a new country. Eli loved to help him out, always inviting him to the lunch table and having conversation with him. When Eli would tell stories about Emmanuel, he would have the biggest smile on his face.

So, when I let Eli read the obituary on my phone, he didn't say much at first. I asked him what he was thinking, and he couldn't understand why the obituary described Emmanuel more like a noun and not like an adjective. In his perspective, it said who he was, but it didn't say WHO he was.

So, I asked, "If you wrote something about him, what you would say?"

Eli replied, "I would say, he didn't know how to be mean."

He didn't just say he was funny, smart, athletic, or that his speaking was hard to understand sometimes. Eli went deeper than that. He saw Emmanuel as a friend. He noticed his character. He went past the color of skin and into the heart. He wanted all the good that he witnessed about his friend to be known for the world to remember.

I will forever treasure Eli's words about his friend. I will always remember how he stood strong and brave at the funeral.

Without knowing it, that sweet boy known as Emmanuel, left behind a legacy that, I pray, leaves a forever impression on my son. "He didn't know how to be mean."

What a way to be remembered.

Lord, it is a beautiful thing to leave a legacy of kindness. Help us Lord be mindful of our actions so those who come after us will carry kindness on into generations to come. Amen!

TODAY'S TREASURES

DAY 36

No longer will you be called Abram; your name will be Abraham, for I have made you a father of many nations.

GENESIS 17:5 (NIV)

FROM FATTER TO FATHER

By: Eric Bivens

The older I get, the more I realize how easy it is to fatten myself with sweets and tasty treats. What used to easily "work itself out" doesn't work itself out like it used to. So recently, I went on a diet and discovered that dieting isn't as easy as it used to be either.

Physically losing weight is very similar to spiritually dying to the self. Both take sacrifice. Both take consistent effort. Both require that we surrender the wants and desires of the world, in order to become lean and healthy.

We are all called to live according to a purpose. God has a plan for each of us. There are times when we get too fat on our own ambitions and need to lose some weight spiritually, so we can be prepared for the plan.

When God called Abram to be the father of many nations, He changed his whole name to Abraham. The physical symbolism of changing his name was to spiritually represent God's promise. In Hebrew, the added "h" to both Abraham (and Sarah too) means, "exalted father, or parent." God knew the purpose and the plan; He wanted Abram and Sara to be known for the promise He had for them.

What is God's plan for you? Do people know you according to God's promise for your life? It doesn't mean you have to change your name, but maybe your diet, and I'm not talking about the physical body. I talking about a spiritual diet. Surrendering to God is a continual, day-by-day exercise of praying, reading God's Word, and acting in faith (some of which is a physical workout for the spiritual soul). Just like dieting physically, if we are consistent to a spiritual diet, we can fight off the selfish desires in order to become strong and healthy in Christ Jesus.

For me, I don't want to be known as "fatter" to my three boys. I want to change one of those t's to an h and be known as "father." I don't want the world to see me as selfishly going after the things of this world, but I want to be known for going after the promises of God.

Lord, I pray for my spirit to be lean and healthy. I want to be strong in you. Keep me encouraged. Just like a physical diet can be tough and take a long time to show results, I pray that my consistency in praying, reading your Word, and acting out my faith will yield in results that people recognize. Today is the start to begin my spiritual diet. I want to be known for your promise unto me.
Amen!

TODAY'S TREASURES

DAY 37

For this world is not our home; we are looking forward to our everlasting home in heaven.

HEBREWS 13:14 (TLB)

HOME

Used to, I always wanted to be doing something out and about, needing to be entertained in some way. Having gotten older, I've gone from a desire to go, go, go, to a longing to be home, home, home. I love my home. I love the people in my home. I love the little details that remind me it's my home. I love the coziness of my home. I love that I'm free to be me in my home. I love that I can find comfort in the still moments of my home.

I walk out the door for work and I already miss home. Even when we go on vacation and have such a good time making the best memories, I'm excited to come back home. After being out in the daily routine of the world going, dealing, handling, coping, listening, solving, and planning – I just want to be home.

No matter how much I love this home, however, it will not last forever. In this home dust still gathers, sickness finds its way in, and grouchiness erupts from the wrong side of the bed every now and then. It will never remain in its original state. Things will have to be replaced, updated, and repaired.

As much as I love my home, there is another home that I already love even more than this one and I've never stepped foot in the door. It's our heavenly home. Jesus is the host. It's always clean. Sickness doesn't exist there. Worship replaces grouchiness.

There is a longing inside each of us for this better place. Like a homesickness that we just can't wait to get back to, even though we've never been. I love The Message version of Romans 8:18, That's why I don't think there's any comparison between the present hard times and the coming good times. The created world itself can hardly wait for what's coming next. Everything in creation is being more or less held back. God reins it in until both creation and all the creatures are ready and can be released at the same moment into the glorious times ahead. Meanwhile, the joyful anticipation deepens.

The perfect contentment I find when I'm home is just a reflection of the full picture of eternity. I get the biggest smile on my face knowing I can live a full life here on earth and there's something even better to come. My forever Home.

Lord, thank you for the hope of heaven. Until that day, may your will be done here on earth as it is in heaven, as we continue to bring you glory in all we do.
Amen!

TODAY'S TREASURES

DAY 37

Love is patient, love is kind. Love does not envy, is not boastful, is not arrogant, is not rude, is not self-seeking, is not irritable, and does not keep a record of wrongs. Love finds no joy in unrighteousness but rejoices in the truth. It bears all things, believes all things, hopes all things, endures all things.

1 CORINTHIANS 13:4-7 (CSB)

LOVE WINS

By: Isaiah Bivens

In the pages of our lives, love emerges as something that brings joy, happiness, and a deeper sense of purpose. Just as the Bible teaches us about the importance of love and connection, our own experiences can reflect the nature of this emotion.

In my life, my relationship with my girlfriend, family, and my close friends has reflected this emotion. The joy I've received from these people and experiences is something nothing else could compare to.

We won't always be as happy with this emotion as we are in other times. But we must remain patient, for love is something that takes time to understand, especially in a relationship with someone else. We will have times of trouble and moments of anger but love always wins.

Lord, we love because you first loved us. Thank you for being the best example. Help us to love like you in all the moments of our day.
Amen!

TODAY'S TREASURES

_____

_____

_____

_____

_____

_____

_____

_____

_____

_____

_____

_____

_____

_____

_____

_____

_____

DAY 39

Go back to your home and tell all that God has done for you.

LUKE 8:39 (CSB)

GOD STORIES

It was the most beautiful summer evening. Plus, it was a Friday! Work was over. The boys had plans of their own, allowing Eric and I a night to eat at our favorite pizza place and a walk by the river. It was beautiful. I love to take advantage of any opportunity to sit outside, and this restaurant has great outside seating.

As we were finishing our meal and enjoying our time, a friend we hadn't seen in a while approached. We were excited to see each other, catch up, and give big hugs. The conversation landed on the topic of church, how ours and hers are both growing, and the wonderful things God is doing. We were coming to a natural end of the conversation, when she said she wanted to share a really cool story with us.

As she started to share, her face was radiant with God's glory. It's not my story to tell, but it was an amazing story about prayer and how God answered a prayer. It was one of those stories that gives you little God bumps all over. We were so delighted to hear her testimony about God's wondrous work! She was simply pouring out her excitement, while at the same time filling us up.

Isn't that what sharing a testimony is about? Allowing others to see and experience all that God can do, so they can be filled with hope and be encouraged that He will do the same for them! Don't hold your God-stories back. The world needs to hear them.

Can you imagine if we didn't have the Bible? It's full of stories and testimonies that have inspired us to press on. Likewise, your story is just an extension of God's continuing works.

Go and tell all what God has done for you.

___

Lord, we should never be at a lack for words when it comes to sharing your goodness. Yet, when we feel weak in our own words, we can find strength in yours. May others find courage by hearing our God stories.
Amen!

TODAY'S TREASURES

DAY 40

Look, I am about to do a something new, even now it is coming. Do you not see it? Indeed, I will make a way in the wilderness, rivers in the desert.

ISAIAH 43:19 (CSB)

FROM THAT TIME ON

When in the middle of a desert season, it's hard to see a testimony on the other side of all the tumbleweeds. Have you ever been there? You feel stuck. You don't know what to do but you feel like God has planted a dream inside you. You wonder what good could come from it, or what to do next. After all, things don't grow in the desert, right? Actually, yes, they do. There are plants and flowers God designed specifically for the desert climate.

In the book of Matthew, chapter 4, Jesus shows us how we can grow from a deserted wilderness to living wild in our calling. For forty days Jesus had been fasting and then the devil started tempting. He tempted him with food, telling him to prove himself, and offering him all the splendor of the world. Jesus batted back every temptation with his Father's Truth. He had spent time with his Father, he knew his Word, and he knew His promises. He had prayed. He was prepared.

After his time in a desert season, that's when it happened. From that time on Jesus began to preach. "Repent, for the kingdom of heaven has come near." There is no testimony without a test. There is no message without a mess. There is no growing without some groaning. There is no passion without the pain of suffering. Jesus probably could have stepped into his public ministry at any time, but I love that he stepped into it after he was tested. It shows his holiness in human form. It shows us what we're truly capable of with God.

Earlier, I mentioned that God designed plants and flowers specifically for the desert, however we are not meant to take root there. We just pass through our desert seasons. I once had my own desert season. It was very quiet and widespread. I would look around and see nothing on the horizon of my hopes and dreams. I thought God was finished with me in the area of ministry. I had no plans to speak. I was experiencing writers' block. I had no idea where to go from there. One day I decided that if this is where He wants me, then this is where I'll stay. I found myself content with the opportunities He had already given and if that was enough for Him, then it could be enough for me. It was in that contentment and trust in the Lord that He started to water the dry and barren places of my soul and new hopes started to bubble up inside me.

I treasure that deserted wilderness. It brought me closer to Jesus, deeper into the Word, and grew me a little bit more spiritually than I was before. He was making a way the whole time, planning for rivers in the desert. As you yourself walk through a desert, know that you are not alone. It may seem quiet but praise Him anyway. It may seem dead, but God brings dead things to life. It may seem motionless, but God is moving.

Lord, give us strength to wait on and trust in you. Help us to embrace every moment – grow us, heal us, and draw us closer to you. Thank you that you are Living Water and with you we will never be thirsty again.
Amen!

TODAY'S TREASURES

WANT MORE?

Visit freeandfancy.com and follow Jodie Bivens on social media

www.ingramcontent.com/pod-product-compliance
Lightning Source LLC
Chambersburg PA
CBHW050906160426
43194CB00011B/2309